Paradise on Earth
with Words

Paradise on Earth with Words

Collection 3:
Love to Live

Eric Scott Grand

Eric Scott Grand has been writing poetry for the last thirty years. He is the author of two earlier books in the *Paradise on Earth with Words* series—*Oceanic* and *Social Society*—as well as a third poetry collection titled *Aspirational Goals*. He has been published in anthologies, attended poetry symposiums, and recorded songs. Grand lives and writes by the majestic Pacific Ocean in Carlsbad, California. This is his fourth collection of poetry.

ericscottgrand@gmail.com

www.ericscottgrand.wixsite.com/website
www.paradiseonearthcollections.com

© 2023 Eric Scott Grand

ISBN 979-8-218-38285-8

Edited and designed by Tell Tell Poetry

Printed in the United States of America

First Printing, 2024

Contents

* * *

* * *

* * *

Acknowledgments

I would like to thank all of the people involved with getting this collection completed. Many of these poems would not have been expressed in their entirety without them.

Paradise on Earth
with Words

Soulmates

They most likely will meet privately when the timing is right in the meantime they wait they're soulmates who have the same interests to get a career position succeed live their dreams to be successful great they're soulmates who want more to feel secure in an environment reassured with large amounts of space they're soulmates

When they both have something in common they have a high compatibility rate they're soulmates with qualities that have similarities that are recognized they're soulmates who share the same values eat food that's whole natural stay fit to lose weight they're soulmates

There will be a moment when they will catch up with each other when they least anticipate they're soulmates if they get together it may happen by an accident that's arranged they're soulmates who find themselves in situations that are coincidences where they can relate they're soulmates

Pure as the Driven Snow

Her skin glows it shows she's pure as the driven snow her body temperature is cold she doesn't look old in a way that most people would pay for she's pure as the driven snow she looks radiant vibrant when outdoors she's pure as the driven snow

Her clothes are pressed clean her appearance is neat in every way shape form she's pure as the driven snow she doesn't have to worry whether she looks pretty when it comes to freshening up just a touch-up is enough with no concerns she's pure as the driven snow she's endowed with good health has habits that are well wherever she goes she's pure as the driven snow

She shines in the light it's noticeable she's pure as the driven snow she is easy to get along with doesn't get upset she is comfortable to be close she's pure as the driven snow she does her best to do what's correct to prosper financially grow she's pure as the driven snow

Looked Upon with Curious Interest

When you've caught someone's attention a friendly gesture is the most likely reaction next when looked upon with curious interest then you may walk towards them to know what's on their mind for sure to give you an opportunity to say a compliment when looked upon with curious interest there may be a reason to get closer to get to know someone if time permits when looked upon with curious interest

Seen across a room that's distant when looked upon with curious interest it can be seen briefly there may be words spoken that are noticed when approached talking is more to know what's going on an introduction can take place with a smile on your face who can be introduced then be amused questions may be asked about a situation when looked upon with curious interest watched closely when feeling lonely it may not last long when passed by till the moment it's interrupted elsewhere in an instant when looked upon with curious interest

When observed from farther away an obvious act would be to see what's going on as a following step when looked upon with curious interest facial expressions body language create mixed signals to give a purpose to speak your opinions when looked upon with curious interest when noticed your motives are questioned if brought up mentioned to find out your intentions when looked upon with curious interest

Love Connections

They're incidents coincidences when put into situations to have more communication that involves a couple with similar interests who get along that doesn't feel wrong who keep looking in each other's direction they're love connections both have professional manners wait to build respect give one another space occasionally walk at a normal pace close then take a quick glance fast for affection they're love connections even though one may not be aware the other looks to notice acts like they're blind however they can see from the corner of their eyes sometimes they'll be near each other make kind gestures to make the other feel better even if they're not able to engage in conversation briefly good sentiments are mentioned they're love connections

They're a series of events that happen by chance but not accidental without intervention they're love connections who are both roughly the same size strength in mind who can have an uncanny resemblance they're love connections when one of them is occupied then there's time that the other thinks is being seen they behave courteous towards one another when caught up in a situation they can handle it with patience when they're love connections

They're moments of concern that may seem important to be noticed if that's your intention they're love connections that include ending up in a pair of two that's normally good when spoken freely that makes it easy to see each other frequently without objections they're love connections it doesn't hurt when there's more support from the people they're closest to receiving their approval that both are suitable to live together without assumptions they're love connections

A Piece of Their Heart

When you're able to be near someone over time know their habits to appreciate who they are for a piece of their heart once you find a connection there's a way to get their attention what happens next is unexpected you're at a loss for what direction to take not wanting to make a mistake it's best to wait keep your distance stay apart for a piece of their heart when you're able to see how a person changes then you're able to reflect on their experience later they say they feel the same it's something two can grow from the start for a piece of their heart

When you're able to observe a person's movements you're able to get to know their character nature mentality personality how smart they are for a piece of their heart what takes place later can't be anticipated with time preparation to beat the odds for a piece of their heart when you're able to know a person's patterns you're aware of their abilities how they respond react when you're around them you stay alert for a piece of their heart

When you're able to see a person's daily routine it's possible to tell how they do well in what they set out to accomplish with no problems to not make it hard on themselves to not harm anyone else when they show respect for a piece of their heart when you're able to be close to someone you're able to find what they're all about their strengths weaknesses what they keep close they hold onto for a piece of their heart when you're able to be around somebody who inspires you who gives consideration accepts who you are shows for a piece of their heart

The Chase

When two people have a connection one believes it but the other won't reveal it one is calm the other is tough who won't share their space it's the chase one likes adventure that's fun the other likes to stay active fit to look young to watch their weight it's the chase one keeps it to themselves the other won't tell anyone else one maintains their distance the other acts innocent one gets the impression the interest will be gone the other believes it will be long when they realize it's the chase

When two people are a perfect match one plays hard to get the other is flirtatious it becomes a cat-and-mouse game it's the chase while one person takes a peek the other plays hide and seek just to see what develops when they wait it's the chase one plays teases to please the other makes it seem they ought to cease one wants to get enough attention so it won't go too far the other doesn't want any problems who at times hesitates it's the chase

When two people are made for each other one acts as though it's all so simple while the other keeps it complicated one tries to be nice while the other has their pride one talks a lot while the other doesn't have much to say it's the chase one tries to get involved the other likes to find solutions solve problems one keeps quiet the other stays silent one knows they have things in common while the other thinks they are complete opposites one would think it's wrong the other knows what they want who approaches with forward steps a chance to take it's the chase

Metro Vice Vixen

On the streets she puts in an early shift law enforcement is her profession she's a metro vice vixen I see her some days she's a short distance away she's not that far she stands on guard in her general vicinity she looks out for criminal activity it's part of her job description she's a metro vice vixen her duty is her highest priority when there are problems she solves them when someone gets hurt she's there to protect serve when someone is in need she's there as the police that's her title position she's a metro vice vixen

She takes strolls on her beat while she's on patrol where she's assigned to stop crime that's part of her present precinct she's a metro vice vixen she prevents violence in a public environment in proximity to a city to do her job as a cop to keep the peace without assistance she's a metro vice vixen who has a routine walking on her feet appointed to stop infractions by handing out tickets she's a metro vice vixen

She does her duty as added security in case of emergency preventing harm that's forbidden she's a metro vice vixen when someone commits a serious offense she places them under arrest when someone doesn't behave appropriately she can escort them off the premises if it's in her best interest she's a metro vice vixen who can be of some assistance when someone's in trouble she's helpful with her protection they won't be a victim she's a metro vice vixen

Fox Hunt

It's a chase to find a mate that involves feelings body chemistry when two people end up in love in a fox hunt one has already taken the bait the other has to wait see what part fate has to play the dominant lover becomes the pursuer by any means possible who follows without trouble he makes her aware that he cares he persists to make sure he exists from a distance not to cause harm in a fox hunt both participants might have the same interest in a field of study that starts as a hobby for them it can be important it means a lot in a fox hunt

It's a challenge to face your fears to be near the person you'll want in your heart in a fox hunt his persistence receives many rejections but it's not bad to try if there's a good reason why to be with someone in a fox hunt it's how you decide who's right to be by your side perhaps find the one who may be your wife in the long run in a fox hunt

It's a test of your courage when you're an expert to be perfect it's mastered eventually to be happy with a person to make it a bit more fun in a fox hunt there might be an age barrier gap however if you work together you can get to know each other better then decide if you want to have an affair that cannot be wrong in a fox hunt it makes us believe that destiny has control of our lives for once in a fox hunt

I Would Like to Get to Know Someone Like Yourself

We've communicated for quite some time through landlines we got to know one another better now I would like to get know someone like yourself to see where it would lead if it's worth the time to continue to date find our way to associate go out often I would like to get to know someone like yourself we felt an attraction that gave us satisfaction that's meant to leave us content to take it to the next step that it would be good if we met not have second thoughts I would like to get to know someone like yourself

We kept in contact by correspondence after which we shared the same interest it's better now I would like to get to know someone like yourself to see what you're like personally to know if we share the same beliefs that we don't think differently if you're in good health I would like to get to know someone like yourself a connection led us in the right direction then we made a decision at a precise moment to make arrangements to get together at an undisclosed location just the two of us not with anyone else I would like to get to know someone like yourself

We wrote about how we felt rather than speaking with words now I would like to get to know someone like yourself to take it to the next level if your appearance is like the picture I've seen when we chat I would like to get to know someone like yourself we discovered we had qualities in common found ways to bond to find out about each other well I would like to get to know someone like yourself

Compatible

With your image my vision we can have a good relationship we work alike energetic that's to be respected that's possible this can make us compatible we have the best intentions that can be mentioned with each other's help it can all work out this can make us compatible how you're driven I'm ambitious we can make a difference that's practical this can make us compatible

With your appearance my perseverance we'd be quite the pair always prepared to show what we know we have potential that's manageable this can make us compatible how you're creative I'm dedicated we'll both be able to show what we're capable of how we're responsible this can make us compatible how you're competitive my work ethic is excessive this can make us bold courageous magical this can make us compatible

With your pursuit of excellence my discipline toward perfection it would be no trouble for us to be a couple we have the same values reaching success isn't impossible this can make us compatible we both show a promise that should be honored ways to provide to be recognized with our combined minds it will all turn out fine if you're willing to take a gamble this can make us compatible how you're knowledgeable I'm understandable we can be the two who make each other's dreams come true in our careers the fields we choose that are profitable this can make us compatible

A Beautiful Person

You're a beautiful person who deserves the best not anything less you're too good for what you're instructed to do you have a routine that's completed with speed you speak your mind to be truthful you're a beautiful person who ought to get what's expected when directed without objections who doesn't need an explanation who looks healthy youthful you're a beautiful person

You're a beautiful person who should get more than what you're worth for the effort put in that's earned you're given a preference in regard to a profession that's dutiful you're a beautiful person who doesn't have to say much to get her point across to be useful you're a beautiful person

You're a beautiful person who has every right to feel entitled to the finest luxuries to have someone cater to your every whim with delicacies that are fruitful you're a beautiful person who should receive what your intention is to seek that's meaningful you're a beautiful person

Only Time Will Tell

Only time will tell when we get to know each other well then we can decide from there if we would like to see each other more first we have to agree to meet then set a date in a comfortable place that we can arrange if we both think it's okay for a meeting to be held only time will tell when it's realized not denied then we'll see each other more often we'll have no doubt about going out only time will tell

Only time will tell when our paths will cross we'll speak to one another about anything we want with no one there to be aware just to be safe we could wait it could be swell only time will tell when it's recognized we acknowledge who we like but we keep our distance currently just for now only time will tell

Only time will tell when it's decided when we will be together somewhere where it's alright that we keep it between ourselves only time will tell when it's concluded not refuted when both of us would be better off to be closer when that's not bad at all only time will tell

On the Same Level

One-time glance there may be a chance two times looked the odds may be good three times seen there's opportunity when both live up to their responsibilities they can be a couple they're able to be together if they believe feel their connection is special when they're on the same level they can try to comply they can behave be nice so issues can be settled when they're on the same level they can split it among themselves a fair share when they're on the same level

The first to communicate sets matters straight the second to talk gives complaints the last to speak leaves you speechless you can only guess what to expect next that will have some sort of effect that will cause a reaction between two people who are able to show affection for each other who like to compete get results when they both measure up it's commendable when they're on the same level they're able to get along without differences that are wrong so they continue to have an interest in common that's not terrible when they're on the same level they can work matters out have a relationship that becomes marital when they're on the same level

Once acknowledged there can be a possible sign of affection twice spoken there's the possibility for compatibility third said they can be close like lovebirds they deserve more when they're on the same level they can operate with what comes naturally to them when they're on the same level they can rely on each other to do what the other wants if it's reasonable when they're on the same level

Close Feelings

It can only go so far if we don't get too involved it can run through our minds but it can't be brought to light keeping us thinking with close feelings it's kept personal can't be shared with anyone who's known there's affection but it can't draw suspicion leaving us speechless with close feelings there are emotions that can't be spoken our concern is to get to know each other more prove that how we feel is real so in secret we keep meeting with close feelings

It can only get to a certain point before there's no return we have to act like usual until our thoughts are mutual when it's safe we can express ourselves how we please with close feelings we have to keep our distance keep talking to a minimum so our true motives will not be discovered that's revealing with close feelings we can't do a lot in public we just live our lives don't look directly into each other's eyes so that others don't question what they see what it might mean with close feelings

It can only reach a certain degree it can't seem obvious for many people to realize with close feelings we can't make grand gestures that draw attention that might later be mentioned we have to keep silent in order not to be apart at the start then later we can decide if we are able to confide in each other to have a good reason with close feelings we have to be professional not let others suspect our true intentions really then when no one's around we can look at each other eventually with close feelings

A Burning Desire that Fuels the Heart

It puts you in a situation where you have to put in the effort to be better in the position to prove what's possible in such a short time that's much needed in moments that are hard it's a burning desire that fuels the heart that makes you find ways to have people look in your direction to have more of an interest not separate grow apart it's a burning desire that fuels the heart making changes with all the necessary preparations set in motion to keep the momentum going to not feel distant far it's a burning desire that fuels the heart

It happens with admiration to give you affirmation for a start it's a burning desire that fuels the heart to capture attention with emotional expression it continues with respect fairness to give consideration show appreciation it allows you to build from there then embark it's a burning desire that fuels the heart it keeps your hopes high to pursue who you're supposed to it means a lot it's a burning desire that fuels the heart

It begins with having a date then two people become one couple where each wants to care for the other so much with every touch it's a burning desire that fuels the heart both get to know one another they share their views opinions strengths weaknesses when they talk together it's a burning desire that fuels the heart then it becomes a relationship to be honest it's better to stay in constant communication to not lose contact it's a burning desire that fuels the heart

Chance Encounter

It can be an event that's time spent by the hour it's a chance encounter when people plan to see each other there is some risk if you're not sure what will occur when the opportunity presents itself about an experience that's to be found out it's a chance encounter that takes place unexpectedly it can continue on the condition it's not spoken about it can cause shock if caught it's a chance encounter

It can be arranged between people who meet discreetly keep it secret don't talk about it to build trust it's a chance encounter to know who you're able to rely on to be in contact later it's a chance encounter that can happen at the last minute it doesn't always end on a positive note it's better to be prepared for the unexpected if any wrongdoing is suspected be alert so you don't get hurt be on guard so you're not harmed it's a chance encounter

It can happen if you take into serious consideration keeping your options open for thrills that count it's a chance encounter your odds would be greater if you're doing something in common if the demographics are correct if the compatibility rating ranks high if the stars align right match up with a person's likeness there can be no doubt it's a chance encounter when you're sure of yourself it's possible it can take place when you're not hesitant negative that can add up it's a chance encounter

Sparks Fly

They're set off like fireworks before they burst in the sky that's when sparks fly they can bring a notion to express emotions if you're with someone it feels magical astronomical seen with your eyes that's when sparks fly they can draw people closer if they enjoy the sight that's when sparks fly

They're ignited when two people are excited when they hold each other close not divided that's when sparks fly they have deep feelings they won't deny that's when sparks fly that tell when they treat each other well to show how much they're liked that's when sparks fly

They're lit like firecrackers when they explode prior to when the smoke recedes rising high that's when sparks fly they might have brought out a thought if the mood was good they're questions that give explanations make us wonder why that's when sparks fly that could be an unexpected reaction surprise that's when sparks fly

Secret Rendezvous

They meet at an undisclosed location on schedule for a secret rendezvous she undresses herself he smiles then he carries her to a resting place then it gets sexual on a secret rendezvous her skin is smooth their eyes align words are exchanged they're now beside each other their hands are tightly gripped constant movement added pressure his whispers relieve her nerves both are pleased when they leave they swear it will be kept on a professional level after a secret rendezvous

They get together at an unannounced spot not to get caught by anyone they know on a secret rendezvous they reveal how they feel they approach closer slower feel tension shivers combined they wonder if it is the moment to show their emotions they pause a bit then continue during a secret rendezvous they indulge in a relationship that can launch from there to be a full-blown affair in situations like this it's better to keep a tight lid on your mouth so it's not talked about outside of a secret rendezvous

They have an encounter at an undetermined area with privacy for sure on a secret rendezvous what they expect is an experience not to forget it will be a memory etched in their minds of the good times on a secret rendezvous they'll look back at the moments they had that were not so bad to ensure they would not say a word it will be kept confidential between the two on a secret rendezvous

Flames of Romance

There's a spark set off when we make love a flame ignites when we smile a fire starts when we hear the beat of our hearts there's a blaze our eyes get wide when we get excited we can feel the heat between the sheets our encounter gets romantic starting from your shoulder I run my hand down your back we have physical contact finally when we've had enough we turn over stare at the ceiling we enjoy the feeling

There's a reaction that happens when we find ways to consummate there's a combustion that sets off an eruption I see your attraction there's an interaction it gets explosive when it's noticed we can sense a tension our sincerity makes us want to have intimacy we hold hands then lead each other to a space that's a comfortable place where we can do so much with each other's touch till we are exhausted at last we've done what we wanted we look up in the direction of the roof it felt good

There's an effect when we have intercourse it gets unbearable when we can't resist when we move closer slowly our body temperatures rise by surprise then we let go there's hot humid air after we're together later when we're done we rest on our backs we see what's above after making love

An Experience to Remember

As the night slipped away I didn't want it to end I wanted this moment to last forever it was an experience to remember we got along well as far as I can tell I won't forget the moments we shared it was an experience to remember our encounter was brief we could not repeat it when I think about this it just makes me more aware it was an experience to remember

As the evening started I didn't want it to be over I wanted it to stay everlasting never finished it was an experience to remember we talked laughed made the hours pass when we think about our lives in the past we recall it was an experience to remember we met for a short amount of time that didn't last much longer than a few seconds we could not do it again but I had no regrets it was an experience to remember

As the dark descended I didn't want it to be done I wanted it to linger on longer together it was an experience to Remember we came in close contact that was incredible memorable that we cherish it was an experience to remember we had no doubts about the outcome we felt better It was an experience to remember

Mutual Feelings

Psychically connected telepathically speaking they're mutual feelings one already knows how the other will react before it happens they know with their senses if they're being noticed they can tell with their instincts if they're being perceived they're mutual feelings they know how the other will act when it comes to pass they can guess their choice preference in a heartbeat before they select it they're mutual feelings

Mentally stable on an emotional level they're mutual feelings they can tell when they're being watched without getting caught one is coy while the other tries to avoid they share similar patterns in speech they're mutual feelings one advises while the other does what's right one comes up with a plan while the other does what's best with the resources they have with intentions for healing they're mutual feelings

Sensitively attuned to one another each one knows when the other is near they're mutual feelings one is aware beforehand while the other knows what to expect next they know even before a question is asked it doesn't have to be asked twice they're mutual feelings for them talk is cheap they prefer to take action rather than speak they're mutual feelings

She's All I Need

She's all I need to complete me to not feel stressful to accomplish to be successful she's all I need to find peace to think equally with her support I can achieve anything she's all I need

She's all I need to keep me happy to know that all my life was not for nothing it meant something deserving rewarding she makes it easier to breathe to have a sigh of relief she's all I need for the effort I've made she will be the prize I've won so I can be number one in a struggle to compete she's all I need

She's all I need to live perfectly in harmony to not feel only lonely give her security not feel weak she's all I need to exist with her near we can be people of means she's all I need

Compatible Match

When two people are meant for each other they're more productive with no drawbacks if they're a compatible match if they have something in common they can function easier to stay on a proper path if they're a compatible match where there's a likeness there can be happiness there are qualities for equality to stay on the right track if they're a compatible match

When two people have constant eye contact they may have an attraction that causes a distraction but they will meet later if they can if they're a compatible match if they have the same interest in living simpler giving each other pointers on how to be quick efficient to lend a helping hand if they're a compatible match if both try to hurry there's less of a worry if there's a lack of security they're not sure where each other have been it gives them somewhere to start in an emergency to find out the facts if they're a compatible match

When two people want to live lives that are alike one's name remains in the back of the other's mind wondering whether it's worth the risk to see if they get along if they're a compatible match if they have feelings that are mutual they each know what the other does they find ways to excel outside their daily routine to advance if they're a compatible match if they both want to improve it isn't wrong what they do won't keep them detached if they're a compatible match

All the Reasons I Love Her

She is fun makes me feel how I emotionally want she tells me what's on her mind I treat her kind she's of the female sex we talk when she has free time available she studies on her own she's determined to reach her goals these are all the reasons I love her

She is young who I spend hours with together long she makes me laugh I show her my gratitude she has a sweet attitude we share our thoughts together we see each other on a daily basis we meet at different locations she fascinates me she's lovely these are all the reasons I love her

She is one who I can trust who occupies my life I show her kindness she gives me no problems we speak on good terms we communicate through words she's the best someone who I'll never forget these are all the reasons I love her

Two of a Kind

We're two of a kind separate individuals who think like one mind with different brains on the same wavelength intuition perceives us a connection is made a situation we're going through seems similar our thoughts sound familiar we're two of a kind separate individuals who think like one mind close yet miles apart a general likeness is found when we're going through a situation we can identify our problems rectify we're two of a kind how we met was no accident how we feel is not coincidence we can relate to resolve any situation we communicate we're two of a kind

True Love

When you've found someone who's a good match who you become attached to who you're not able to stop thinking of that's true love it makes you inspired to reach higher you feel energized not tired who gets your attention to make an impression who you're not able to get enough of that's true love when you've seen somebody who has similarities that's meant to be who you're not able to leave the thought of that's true love

When you've realized who you're intended to be with then you're not able to see that person with anyone else only with yourself if you let the person know don't talk to anyone else too much then do what's expected of that's true love who does whatever it takes who goes to great lengths not to wait who you don't want to let go of that's true love when you know for sure who you're able to relate with you're able to find ways to communicate messages to convey who's right to be with not separate who you're sure of that's true love

When you've come to discover who is most suitable with qualities that are mutual who you're not able to stop talking of that's true love who motivates you to be creative to take action to get a reaction to show what you're made of that's true love when you're able to identify with a person who shares a likeness who has a thirst for knowledge makes decisions these characteristics that you've always dreamed of that's true love

Love

Affection matters between two people when their bodies are up close from head to toe they hold each other in their arms they're in love they look into each other's eyes their skin touches they're in love glances are exchanged the attraction between them is the signal they send they're in love

There has to be an agreement when opposites attract from top to bottom so it forms a bond when they're in love they stand close with an embrace to carry each other's weight they don't scare easily they're not likely to run off when they're in love they take one step closer with each heartbeat to discover what they want most when they're in love

Mutual respect must be present that's an arrangement that gives equal treatment to two people from above to below where both won't be harmed when they're in love they're near where they can hear each other breathe they feel sure secure comfortable have trust when they're in love they look at one another have some eye time then say what's on their mind talk with their mouths to help each other out when they're in love

Love to Live

There's a reason to procreate to show affection for a marital relation to make sense it's love to live for personal growth rest assured you're secure in what you've got to give it's love to live you have a purpose to reproduce after a matrimonial ceremony to have kids it's love to live

It makes you feel great puts a smile on your face makes it seem like your problems are gone when there's that special someone to be with it's love to live you can move forward be nurtured grow stronger aware that your life will be longer be reassured you won't feel any regrets for the things you did it's love to live that puts you in a mood that's good that leaves an expression that makes you grin it's love to live

It leaves you happy that's a moment of contentment that your well-being is guaranteed you can do as you please easily without a hitch its love to live you find peace prosperity harmony without guilt about to forgive it's love to live when it keeps getting better when you don't want the time to end it's love to live

Amends

We were close not separate then somewhere in between it got to the point we were mean to each other our love was put to the test based on this can we make amends let's forget what was said to move ahead let's improve not be rude not abuse have a truce it would be better if we were together let's put the past to rest based on this can we make amends we started as friends it got serious as time passed by we thought alike it felt right then somewhere along the line we stooped to insult it might've been both of our faults based on this can we make amends

We were inseparable never apart then we started to get busy we got impatient restless when I tried to make up for it I gave you gifts based on this can we make amends can we forget what we did before then continue onward not make the same mistakes under these circumstances can we show some respect based on this can we make amends when we were kind to one another we felt no harm after some time it became distressing to not be alarmed we gave each other space when we could not come in close contact to talk then realized we could change forgive find a way to live not pretend based on this can we make amends

We were tight not divided then somewhere down the road we grew tired of the old our relationship was on the line based on this can we make amends can we just not recall what we did return to normal not feel hurt based on this can we make amends we began as companions then our lives took a turn for the worse we could not control later on we still felt the same we were not to blame based on this can we make amends

Signs of Affection

When times were simple I got the necessities I needed with no questions asked I would return the gesture with a smile

When times were easy I got whatever needed all I did was ask I would return the gesture with a hug

When times were good I got the gifts I needed unexpectedly without asking I would return the gesture with a kiss

Lucky in Love

It's faith taking a chance destiny finding a match that looms from above when you're lucky in love the world seems much better you're aware what direction you're headed with the one who makes it beautiful who happens to be your companion you'll get what you want when you're lucky in love there's never a dull moment you're cheerful it makes life meaningful nothing can go wrong there will be no grudge every day can be fun when you're lucky in love

It comes from within body chemistry plays a part when you're lucky in love the future seems much brighter when you know for sure how to proceed forward there's no mistake made when you've found your soulmate who touches your heart when you're lucky in love you know it won't get any worse cause you're reassured about who you're meant for you won't stay apart when you're lucky in love

It's hope giving a glance fate creating a challenge to be charming smooth to make your move to show what you've got to be on top when you're lucky in love you've got someone else other than yourself for moral support that doesn't hurt who is somebody you've found who does no harm when you're lucky in love there isn't a boring time when all is fine you're happy with who you've chosen to belong to when you're lucky in love